What critics and writers are saying about *Desert Light*

This is a powerful and perceptive collection, not to be missed.
—Ann Howells, author of *Under a Lone Star,* and editor of *Illya's Honey*

"Meet me between the slashed syllables of in/ex/plic/a/ble," poet Loretta Diane Walker writes, "where even the dripping faucet wants/ to be the Rio Grande . . . singing across borders." Through compelling terrain both earthy and spiritual, sundry lives emerge overlaid with mystery. Vivid, searching poems like these elicit our shared sorrows, hopes, sensibilities. And horizon-wide, they evoke compassion wherein *vulnerability is our light.*
—Laurie Klein, author of *Where the Sky Opens*

What is striking about *Desert Light* is that the "traditional" Southwest poems are *human*, i.e. "a chorale of clouds," "night shuts its ears," "the wind walks quietly," "the sky is a woman," while the poems that are written in first person or second person are more *organic*. You would think it would be the other way around, but this combination becomes an elegant melding of wide-open spaces and interiors. Some of the poems are heartbreakingly tragic but written with such finesse, they catch you by surprise and take your breath away. For every little girl trying to grow up with one shred of dignity and self-esteem, "When I Thought I was Pretty" will give you a name for the lady whose "savage smile could peel skin from stones." "A Dear John Letter On Behalf of My Dignity" should be required reading for everyone. Walker has knocked it out of the park with this quiet, yet powerful and lovely group of poems. You will not be disappointed.
—Tobi Alfier, Co-editor, Blue Horse Press and San Pedro River Review

So you think you've heard the moon described every way possible and you've read every sky description possible. Well, you are wrong. Tuck into this achingly beautiful work by Walker, where the moon can pole vault, and the sky is a woman. A stunningly wonderful piece of work by a talented poet.
—Michelle Hartman, Author of *The Lost Journal of my Second Trip to Purgatory* and editor, *Red River Review*

Desert Light

Desert Light

Loretta Diane Walker

LITERARY PRESS
LAMAR UNIVERSITY

ISBN: 978-1-942956-45-7
Library of Congress Control Number: 2017952267

Book design: Salena Parker

Lamar University Literary Press
Beaumont, Texas

For my mother and rock
Mary A. Walker

Recent poetry from Lamar University Literary Press

Bobby Aldridge, *An Affair of the Stilled Heart*
Michael Baldwin, *Lone Star Heart, Poems of a Life in Texas*
Charles Behlen, *Failing Heaven*
Alan Berecka, *With Our Baggage*
David Bowles, *Flower, Song, Dance: Aztec and Mayan Poetry*
Jerry Bradley, *Crownfeathers and Effigies*
Jerry Bradley and Ulf Kirchdorfer, editors, *The Great American Wise Ass Poetry Anthology*
Matthew Brennan, *One Life*
Paul Christensen, *The Jack of Diamonds is a Hard Card to Play*
Christopher Carmona, Rob Johnson, and Chuck Taylor, editors, *The Beatest State in the Union*
Chip Dameron, *Waiting for an Etcher*
William Virgil Davis, *The Bones Poems*
Jeffrey DeLotto, *Voices Writ in Sand*
Chris Ellery, *Elder Tree*
Mimi Ferebee, *Wildfires and Atmospheric Memories*
Larry Griffin, *Cedar Plums*
Ken Hada, *Margaritas and Redfish*
Michelle Hartman, *Disenchanted and Disgruntled*
Michelle Hartman, *Irony and Irreverence*
Katherine Hoerth, *Goddess Wears Cowboy Boots*
Lynn Hoggard, *Motherland*
Gretchen Johnson, *A Trip Through Downer, Minnesota*
Ulf Kirchdorfer, *Chewing Green Leaves*
Laozi, *Daodejing*, tr. By David Breeden, Steven Schroeder, and Wally Swist
Janet McCann, *The Crone at the Casino*
Erin Murphy, *Ancilla*
Laurence Musgrove, *Local Bird*
Dave Oliphant, *The Pilgrimage, Selected Poems: 1962-2012*
Kornelijus Platelis, *Solitary Architectures*
Carol Coffee Reposa, *Underground Musicians*
Jan Seale, *The Parkinson Poems*
Steven Schroeder, *the moon, not the finger, pointing*
Carol Smallwood, *Water, Earth, Air, Fire, and Picket Fences*
Glen Sorestad *Hazards of Eden*
W.K. Stratton, *Ranchero Ford/ Dying in Red Dirt Country*
Wally Swist, *Invocation*
Jonas Zdanys (ed.), *Pushing the Envelope, Epistolary Poems*
Jonas Zdanys, *Red Stones*
Jonas Zdanys, *Three White Horses*

For information on these and other
Lamar University Literary Press books go to
www.Lamar.edu/literarypress

Acknowledgments

Many thanks to the editors of the following journals for publishing some of the poems in this collection.

Allegro & Adagio Literary Journal
Amarillo Bay Literary Journal
Aries Literary Journal
Bearing the Mask: Southwestern Persona Poems
A Book of the Year: Poetry Society of Texas
Boundless, The Anthology of the Rio Grande Valley International Poetry Festival
Carrying the Branch: Poets in Search of Peace
Connecticut River Review
Concho River Review
di-vêrsé-city: Anthology of Austin International Poetry Festival
Emily, An Anthology of Dickinson Inspired Work
Encore: Prize Poems
The Enigmatist
A Galaxy of Verse
Ginosko Literary Journal
Haight-Ashbury Literary Review
Harp-String Poetry Journal
Homestead Review
Illya's Honey
Kind of a Hurricane Press
Lifting the Sky: Southwestern Haiku & Haiga
Nomad's Choir
Pennsylvania Prize Poems Anthology
Pushing Out the Boat Literary Journal
Red River Review
River Poets Journal
San Pedro River Review
Songs of Eretz Review
The Southern Poetry Anthology, Volume VIII: Texas
The Stray Branch Literary Journal
Sugared Water Literary Journal
Switchgrass Literary Journal
Yellow Chair Review

I much appreciate Diane Frank for her mentorship, insight, encouragement, support, and friendship; and Barbara Saxton for her feedback, support, and friendship. I'm grateful to Laurie Klein, William Wright, and my friend, Jax for the feedback on several of these poems. I extend my gratitude to Lisa Toth Salinas for building my website and for encouragement, support, and friendship; to Nancy Clark for reading this manuscript, providing feedback, and her continued support of me; to Barbara Blanks for her support; to Cindy Huyser for her editorial skills, encouragement and support; to James Walker, Vincent and Ernie Walker, Mark and Kimberly Schiff; to Chris Walker for the author photo; and to Raymond and Glenda Walker for their constant support and encouragement.

Contents

III. Storms and Starlight

I. Dawn

Dawn

An exiled windmill stares,
refuses to turn its head
as dawn, light's chaste sister,
streaks sky's soft upper lip with orange.

Dew falls on the red *Radio-Flyer*
that waits for children who will not return.
The air sweetens its breath with honeysuckle.
There is goodness in this break of day.

Waking

The future rises
like dawn from a husk of darkness.
And the light is a low wattage bulb.
Somewhere a rooster unpacks sleep
from the trunk of its voice.

We yawn with all of our past tomorrows
tumbling from our breaths, mistake them for morning.

Falling into Morning

It's evident the wind's descending into madness;
scalped maples and oaks manifest in psychosis.

A lone leaf of white paper in a field
overgrown with tumbleweeds flies towards shelter.
An empty green bean can rolls until it finds refuge
underneath a parked car.

Glassy teeth of wind-chimes chatter fearful melodies.
The trees are too traumatized to stop shaking.
Their trembling limbs incessantly thrash against air,
leaves fall into morning.

Is it mad to say there is beauty in the wind's insanity?
The way it forces the day to press its shivering hands
against window screens?

Or the way it drags fallen leaves to a far corner
of the yard, sandwich them between concrete and sky,
their scarlet-orange bodies heaped into a chilly flame?

Summer of ' 68

My cousin, Bobby, throws me in the deep
end of a pool.
I fail to remember what I learn the first day
of swimming lessons, flail my arms
instead of stroke, forget how to paddle my feet.

Water is a heavy lid pressing down on me;
I do not touch bottom.
I kick hard, bob-up gasping, reach for a pole,
listen to spectators laugh.
Chlorine and joking sting the sky out of my eyes
when I shut them, go back under.

I wet myself; feel the burn of fear—shame
on my legs when a strong hand hoists
me onto hot concrete.
I want to go home; my brothers are not ready.
I cower in a corner, stare at the roof
of the Village Market Grocery Store.

I do not think about my cousin, Curtis,
sweating in the jungles of Vietnam,
bullets tearing through Bobby Kennedy,
the Beatles' "Revolution" and "Hey Jude".

My mind blisters with anger.
Biting my bottom lip,
I mentally rehearse punishment
for Bobby. The pungent taste
of revenge ferments on my tongue.
The desire to get him back, rising
like a fresh loaf of bread.

When I Thought I Was Pretty

I wore the colors of earth and clouds:
a homemade gingham dress, white lace socks,
second-hand two-toned patent leather shoes.

I sat on a pew, tapped my new pretties
in rhythm with the hallelujahs and amens
that rippled across the church.
That small scratch on the toe could not dim
the shine of joy that hugged my feet.

A lady with more money than my mother
eyed my eight-year old frame.
"How come your mama let you wear those ugly shoes?"

She grinned at me,
that savage smile could peel skin from stones,
grow a forest of doubt in the limbs
of a breaking child.

Rewind

Sweet Destiny is the color of breakfast,
a cinnamon toast girl with broken wings.
This morning we watch hail bruise the sleepy city.

She leans her head on my shoulder;
her next words sear.
"I can bridle the past around a bale of secrets."

She retreats from me,
returns to her white rooms of silence.
This is how she keeps her mind
from storms and feral hooves.

Child, let me tunnel backwards through time,
unfurl those fists that crushed your temple,
reverse that moment the darkness invaded
every gully of your bones, blood, breath.

The Day My Brother Cried

The frame of our mutt's door is a black hole,
half-full water bowl a cistern of absence.

I come home after my brother searches,
find her white stiff body near the back gate

with untenanted eyes, mouth open,
tongue drooping a final benediction.

Silence weeps on cream carpet,
sobs muffled by shabby fibers.

He gives the quiet his tears,
jumps the hurdle of manliness

to honor the joy she places at his feet.
He stares into the day's soft neck,

voice rough with anger.
I hear a crack in the cup of his throat,

sadness breaks him.
"I know that sorry excuse of a man poisoned her."

He makes a vow, threatens tomato vines, clothesline poles,
bars on the windows, but never the neighbor

who growls at life and foreigners on his lawn.
My mother's wisdom tempers him.

"You can't prove it." She knows, I know
revenge crawls through his body.

Night hides from her shadow,
my brother walks up and down the street

with our mutt's innocence leaning
on the broad shoulders of his promises.

Shades of Gold

I am a goddess.
A tornado's gold
walls spin
in the porcelain's white universe
created in our only bathroom.
Pine-Sol's pungent scent
is a heavy cloud hovering over my
head.
Headstrong with ten years,
I release my wrath from the heavy economy-size bottle.

Liquid streams over toilet,
sink, tub, floor.
I cough,
choke on my own anger.
Why am I the one
on bended knees
making circular motions
with an old torn dirty blue towel?
Why must I clean
what my brothers stain with their yellow ink?

Beans and Birthrights

> He said to Jacob, "Quick, let me have some of that red stew! I'm
> famished!" (That is why he was also called Edom.) Jacob replied,
> "First sell me your birthright."
> —Genesis 25:30-31 (NIV)

When my head broke through the flush light of birth,
you grasped my heel, tried to return me
to the dark plot of your desires.
Father preferred me, mother you,
a strong wedge.
We both skirt the edge
of that river and study each other's weaknesses.

When the feral dog of hunger roamed inside me,
I sold what I could not hold to leash him.
You bought my first cry with a pot of beans.
I left your table full with lentils.
You left our home with my hate
hanging over your head.

When you were a smear on the horizon,
you sent me bleating gifts of fear:
camels, cows, bulls, donkeys.
It was not their blood, bones and flesh I desired;
it was yours. I wanted to feel the strong pulse
of your heart thrumming against the allayed walls of mine.

Museum of Memory

1
In my mind's museum,
violence and weeds are obsolete.
Clocks have no hands.
Tomorrow is a slow current.

Water and a nimbus of light
fill the gallery of my birth.
I am wild with impatience,
rush to swim through
my mother's womb.

When she speaks my name
into the universe,
happiness puts on running shoes,
chases my faint scent.
It has no straight line
to me. I wobble through the years
regretting, reliving, remembering
rejoicing in the artifacts of my life.

2
Memory returns me to Betsy McCall's flat world
where innocence is two dimensional.
Glee plays on my tongue
when my six-year old coffee-colored hands
cut segregation's polite and glossy wardrobe
from the magazine.
I dress paper dolls
with cotton-candy-colored cheeks
and hair the shade of summer wheat.

After humming "Jesus Loves the Little Children",
I tell my white paper sisters stories
of three bears, a sleeping beauty and a red-hooded girl.
I do not have beautiful black fairytales.

3
The sun slow dances over a carpetless floor.
Baskets of September heat hang from high windows.
I am fifteen; the band hall's wooden doors squeal open.
My brother walks forward, face lined with a smile,
a saxophone case dangling in his right hand.
The band plays Happy Birthday.
I am drenched in swells of surprise.
I try to flood my voice with words;
my throat is a gutter of joyful tears.

4
Curious how the body stuffs itself with time,
cannot feel the difference between old and new.
A fist of wind and scratch of light
on the bedroom window
rouse me from shuffling
through these decades of recollections.

There is nothing like the traffic of memories.
There is nothing like the bread of dreams.

A Soldier's Postcard to the Future

In memory of Clarence Edwin "Ed" Hall, a Captain in Air Force Intelligence

Standing on tomorrow's long ledge
gazing through the flag's fifty bright eyes,
will you remember me
when the blood of my blood is etched in stone?
How will I be remembered
when death flushes life from my flesh?

Wars rise
like infected lesions on skin.
Life, liberty, death all bleed
the color of poppies.
Valor is not a silk handkerchief.
It's a tear-clogged throat, a white tombstone grave.
I wear the uniform of ages,
a soldier dressed in history's many battles.
Write my name here:_____
The rain cannot wash it away.

Somewhere the dark, the moon
drops a heavy white period into the night sky.
A broken mother plays "Taps" on the clarinet.

Loss of an Alma Mater

For Ector High School

The shape of our memories—an eagle,
each name a feather on its strong body.
We soar in solitude toward the winter

of our past. We fly from the four corners
of time seeking our home, find a fight song
with broken lyrics, emblems of glory
chucked in dumpsters.

We feed each other our sadness.
Our ghosts too pale for the youthful voices
crowding the halls.
They talk over our history
and the parts of us we left behind.
Our fingers are talons clinging to withering limbs.

The deep chambers of our bodies are blue and white.
These new walls bear the same colors;
should we smear them with our thumbs, whisper
to the unassuming air "remember us?"

Or should we collect quarters, gather them
like fruit in the baskets of our aged hands?
If we press tightly, maybe we can feel
their wings bringing us back to each
other again, and again, and again.

Halloween Costume

> "I have seen my kid struggle into the kitchen in the morning
> with outfits that need only one accessory: an empty gin bottle."
> —Erma Bombeck

"I'm too old for that."
Her attitude, a hilt of teenage snobbery.

Twelve Halloweens swim under the water
of the past; the black pointed witch's hat,
orange velour pumpkin, the princess trio—
Snow White, Cinderella, Sleeping Beauty dresses
form rectangular creatures of memory,
float in the flat glossy corals of photo albums.
She plops in front of a mirror, fingers a palette
of eye-shadow, sweeps her lids with green powder.

When she swathes her pimply face with makeup,
it morphs two shades lighter than her juvenile skin.
She knots the tail of a white T-shirt,
exposes a ribbon of belly flesh,
scissors a pair of faded jeans
with the care little girls use when cutting paper dolls.
Small slits uncover the blooming of her body.
A tide of silence fills the room when she unveils
this year's costume; *I'm a rock star.*
We stare like fish.
Shock nibbles into her Daddy's diplomacy.
"You are not going out like that!"

She wobbles down the sidewalk
on a pair of chunky-heeled shoes,
body shining in anger, costume hidden
beneath the long white shirttail of her daddy's love.

A Poet's Breakfast

For Tobi Alfier

She empties the box of Alpha-Bits Cereal
onto her kitchen table.
The slick mahogany is a threshing tool
as vowels and consonants scatter
like tares and wheat.
She ignores the stray letters at her feet
as she sits and watches the sun slide
from underneath the covers of dawn.
It slips on a long necktie of light,
primps in the bare living-room window.

With a full smile on her face, she selects twelve letters,
scoops the remaining ones back into the box.
Now her hands sprout poems
out of everything she touches—
the frayed cuffs on her mother's cotton blouse,
the cracked tea cup peeking over the edge of the counter,
the carcass of an old red concordance.

The house yawns with noises of waking children.
The floor beneath their tiny feet
sounds like beans snapping.
Sleep leaps out of their voices like small toads,
"Mom-my."
She boils water for tea, retrieves the twelve letters,
pours each child's name in the cold white milk of morning.

Why I Came to the Funeral Drunk

This eulogy, propaganda for my pain,
words wasted on me.
Even now with sorrow scaling the air,
my mind is a megaphone shouting,
berating me for failing, only two drinks.

I try to think about this happiness:
my umbilical cord pumping protection
in the wet world of my womb where he grows.

Months are nine hands ripping him from me,
thrusting him on a path I cannot follow.
One day he is a toddler dragging
a blanket across my feet,
his independence waddling behind.
One day he is a teenager dangling
car keys, trying to hypnotize me with his joy.
One day he is a man dodging
bullets and shrapnel; I try to dodge the bottle.
Today the American flag, a pall on his coffin.
This black dress, tradition. Mourning is colorless.

Greedy Death, fresh as the first fruit of light,
reminds what I grasp with both hands
and grinding teeth is a vapor.
Casting eyes in my direction, it mocks
me the way they do.
How can she? She lost him to one!
They think tearless eyes and the pale yellow liquor
swooshing around my spirit make me a drunk.
I am sober with grief.

Death! I am coming for you. That's what a mad mother does.
That's what a good mother does—go after that which
puts her child in a deep hole of hard clay, buries it like a bone.

Into the Woods

For Laurie Klein

"Hansel, why are you stopping and looking back?"
—Jacob and Wilhelm Grimm

The sun, a white tambourine,
softly shakes heat across the sky.

A boy walks out of the woods,
dark-haired with long rambling legs,
fear towing him forward.

His sister emerges, arms pedaling,
face framed with fury,
voice a soft whip; *Oh, save it!*

I enter the path where they exit, make my
way to Redwood Creek.
A fallen leaf floats in its gentle mouth,
anchors against an island of wet stones.

I pick it up, a gift from the universe.
My fingers shudder with grief when it crumbles
in the small town of my hand.
Such sadness in this little village of darkness.

Hidden in the Light

My body drinks in cocktails of chemo,
burns from the thin red cross of radiation,
while I eat from a table of fear.

Do I do laundry, gas the car before ice dresses
the streets with its slick coat
or plan a vacation I cannot afford?
Details that become blurred
when the double-barrel
of cancer is aimed at my breast.
When the buck shots of those cells splinter,
spread underneath my skin,
a surgeon cuts them out.
Her hands steady even though a week ago
she lost her husband in a cave of water.

I eat from the same table where life,
that hairy-foot mystery, attempts to hide.
What foolishness!
Does it not know its extremities are exposed,
the smallest of its secrets too large to conceal?
With catlike caution, I amble towards its stillness,
wait for its limp hand to move.
Wait for its next surprise.

When the Doctor Said You Have Cancer

For Katie Russell

My larynx was a candle.
A flame of silence burned
in my vocal cords.
Words were silhouettes
on the walls of my throat.
Tears lost the directions to my eyes.

Immortality shrank
from the size of a wide blue day
to a patch of dry twigs.
Fear walked in me with heavy boots
and a hazmat suit, settled
behind a tiny door in my stomach.

I emailed my diagnosis
to a warren of friends, family.
The news mushroomed,
a cloud of dejection drifted
through my outbox,
reached a lady I didn't know.

Through the cloud, her muted voice
circled back to me.
"Hi, Loretta. I am Naomi's friend.
I had cancer. Will you give
me your address?
I want to send you something."

Caution was an abandoned warehouse.
I didn't rehearse the ritual of my childhood.
With fifty-five key strokes,
I unlocked my front door to a stranger,
emailed my address. I wanted her past tense;
anonymity lost its sacredness.

After seven moons passed, the package arrived.
After I lost my hair, my hands remembered:
the compliant of tangles, the silt of shampoo,
intersection of strands that created braids,

a stranger's gift of books, scarves, nightcap, her note.
When I slept in the nightcap, tears found their way
to the hill of my steroid-puffed cheeks.

From the Darkness

Summer, a long tongue of orange
rolls back into the sky.

From my patio, I watch dusk swallow
the last scraps of twilight,
blue banish beneath a mouth of darkness.
My neighbor walks and sings to her mutt
in a seal-colored night.

Fueled by fifteen frustrating dry days,
a storm stalks about snarling.
A timid pale moon shrinks in fear
behind a wall of pewter clouds.
A used white napkin struggles for survival
in the barbaric grip of a merciless wind.

Cancer is the storm in my breast.
Like the napkin, I struggle
in fear's strong current.
Like the moon, I cower
under the cover of sleep,
slip into a rainless dream

where melancholy is a lost gym shoe
in the back of my dark closet
wedged between brown loafers
and black pumps.
With empty eye laces and open mouth,
it moans until the overhead light is a sock of joy
filling its empty sole.

Morning, I move from room to room,
in search of my other self.

This Is What I Want to Give You

For Michelle Hartman

Clouds collapse, clog the night with clammy air.
Long hairs of light loll over a cheek of moon.
I sit on my patio grieving over a knee injury
and the cancer camped in my body.

How subtle the chrysalis of grief,
the way it changes to anger.
I rage at a squirrel traipsing up a tall pine,
at a chorus of coos and screeches in the backyard,
at this gaudy blouse of fear clinging to my breasts.

M, I do not write to drape you with my sadness.
I want to tell you I've made two scrapbooks
with every card, note, banner or piece of encouragement
I received.

Because I could not fit the balloons, I place their pictures
in pictorial nosegay of colors. And in pasting
I notice there is a white butterfly fluttering
around the moonflowers on the other side of my patio.
I hope you can picture it. That is the image
I want to leave with you and me for the coming days.

From a Town as Small as Muleshoe, Texas

On the path to her popularity,
she slams bottles of spirits.
The clock's metal hands
move toward last call.

Her judgment dashes down
the dark alley of no return.
She buys another round of approval;
her stool-mates heads bop yes to the beat.

She flips quarters with her tuition funds,
trades books for beers,
believes she is one of them now—
one of those girls who move in circles

that make others dizzy with envy.
Waning smoke, dwindling chatter,
mammoth silent speakers
compete for false promises of friendship.

Memories of music pound
in the back of her ears.
She sits alone at the bar,
top littered with bottles.

Her stool-mates backs
are a mockery of her innocence/delusions.
They walk away, do not wave or look back.
Their laughter is a dart,

reaches the bull's-eye of her stomach
as she watches them
spill out, become shadows.
She staggers into the faded night

with an empty wallet, heart.
The wind taps a gentle rhythm
on the drum of her cheeks.

The sun frames the nightclub's blue neon sign.
She leans on the loneliness of morning,
eyes leaking tears,
even the moon has abandoned her.

Seduction

You are the most calculating, unfeeling,
inconsiderate, self-centered lover I have known.

You plunge ahead, not waiting for me,
as though you are in charge of the future,
director— caretaker of my happiness
which will not happen if you are not there.

Have you no shame?
I've bartered, compromised, cheated—
yes cheated, to get more of you.

Where do I fit in your life?
You treat me like all others;
even after I said how special you are!
I hear the desire, familiarity in their voices.
It makes me jealous hearing them droning;
they would do this or that with you.
Those things will make you a hostage;
I want to hold, cuddle you like new life.

Do you wear a crystal smile,
show your gold plated-teeth
or squeeze your oversized ego into an ebony hat,
sweep your hands as though you are offering the world
when you seduce lusting women?

Yesterday I watched you change like a chameleon,
flirt with—charm the sky until its big bright cheek
blushed into a million wagging tongues of light.
Now you blink at me with blood-shot eyes,
say—It's 6:30 AM.
Oh, Time, my darling,
I will forgive all of your indiscretions—
flirting, wandering, arrogance
if you give me another hour with you
in the folds of these warm blue covers.

Lament of a Catalpa

Last night I was fence posts.
Taut barbwire cut through my limbs,
my cries covered by wailing wind.
Who will grieve with me?
The cypress? The cedar?
I watch them lift their leafy hands in praise,
shake them with green gratitude
because they are still standing.

The night before I was railroad ties
with my soul splintering as I tasted the trains'
coal broiled breakfast, felt their steel wheels
churn across my trunk.
The Creator wrung clouds like cleaning rags.
The aroma of fresh rain could not wash away
the stench of their motoring.

Who will mourn for me? This coruscant
May morning? The child leaning
against my rough body, reaching
for my ripe fruit? The hummingbirds
on holiday in the folds of my flowers?

Each night when the moon meanders
through the doorframe of darkness,
I dream the scarred arm of history,
the future rising like dawn,
feel the blade of the past
chopping at my strength.

Taken

Songbirds sing through the cage of my ribs
a melody of the beginning.
This is the origin of beauty— bone and dust
taken from the hard side of clay.
He sleeps, cannot deny my birth.
He wakes, feels his sutured side,
learns the meaning of want
in the early morning of a seasonless day.

Grazing wild beast and flying fowl watch as I am taken
from and to the husband of earth.
He laughs, names me wo-man, born of his wound.
And this is what comes from birth— woe, joy,
tears from the pain of tearing, joining
flesh, bone, breath in the steady hands of God.

Light Dripping

Light drips from dawn's leaky faucet.
The sun, too lazy this time of morning
to open the handle.
If it knew the tongue of Juarez,
the heat of its language,
the burn of its dance,
maybe it would not wait
for the mist's delicate hands
to cool all that is fire.

A red-headed woodpecker,
brave in its desires,
drums a love song
into the meekness of day.
Its melody dares the sun to squeeze
fully the white spout of its brawn.

And the two of us, palm to palm,
say hello.
You with life lines forming,
me with lines maturing.
We smile a language
only the two of us understand—
a dialect born from urgency.
We speak it now, with dawn's light
dripping in our lonely fingernails.

And Then

W, we'll gather again Tuesday,
after the resurrection of twilight,
after the A-Train clackety-clacks
into the shapeless bronze horizon
and my daughter stops washing her hair
in the baptismal pool of her tears
because the boy who used to rake
dead leaves from *our* garden
said the magic is gone between them
and he feels fire in the gully of his
bones, blood, breath, and the moon beats
in his chest when he watches *X* walk
through the city in her red mini,
butt rotating like two planets
in a sky seeded with stars.
I tell her love awakens the first layer of our lives;
the heart has pebbled-stones, people come, go—
sadness is like this, too.
And then, without a whimper, she drags out
letters *Y* wrote last year on whiskey-colored paper,
tosses his words in the dark jungle of this week's garbage,
announces in her elegant voice, "This is *Z*."
"He's from Orlando, before that Charleston."
There is no somberness in the seams of her skin,
no need to fill her mouth with violets.
W, let's gather before Tuesday under the white
canopy of morning; we can listen to bluebirds gossip
about the years of decay scaling the backyard gate.

Feeling like the Number 9

For Cindy Huyser

"The 9 lives in the world and understands the connections between
all of mankind. It is a humanitarian..."
—Hans Decoz

"The number 9 symbolizes divine completeness or conveys the
meaning of finality."
—The Bible Study Site

9 with its charitable cistern of compassion
soaks up sun as its head tilts towards the ceiling of sky.
Curious the way its spout constantly points
to the end /beginning of something.

Bridge between different stages of my life, 9.
As a pre-adolescent, it wags its thin tail at me,
a reminder it's the last single digit to conquer
before acquiring the bragging rights of ten.

Twice nine and I'm voting;
freedom is a pair of headlights.
Nineteen in its cheerfulness rolls
across the unkempt field of 20.

29, I feel stability's strong itch,
desire for motherhood, mortgage—
a loud mantra.
30 whirls in debris of disappointments.

39, my emotions— tempestuous winds.
Motherhood is not my calling.
There are no children
to wear the hood of my face.

I grab 40 with the fortitude of the desert,
change the portfolio of my dreams.
Blood of my blood—impossible.
Poems are my offsprings.

9 a.m., this desert air feels like a tight turtle-neck
and I feel like the number 9
with the completion of my 49th year.

There is serenity in the finality of a decade.

I wake in this 9th month, my birthday month,
on this 6th day, with morning light
chiseling through the window.
50 gracefully pours itself in the cup of my body.

How wonderful the way this day hugs me,
does not judge the years dissolving inside my thighs,
crawling around my eyes. How beautiful
the way 9 coils into a shell,
buries itself in my hands' tiny dry rivers.

Death is Not the Only Widow Maker

He wore two masks: the oilman by day,
The Music Man by night. She sliced tomatoes for both.

He performed in the theater of their lawn,
ran his lines while running the hose, pruned his diction
the way he clipped the edges of their hedges, perfectly.
The tomatoes went unpeppered on his plate.

He followed Thespis, wore his shoes and hat,
made her sing "Seventy-Six Trombones"
until the curtain of sleep closed her eyes.
For two months she washed the laundry of a ghost,
found his dirty dishes in the sink, read his script
while she ate the tomatoes.

A Brutal Beauty

For Ann Howells

There is
no contrition
from the cacti; their sharp
language, each thorny syllable,
planned pain.

early morning light
a red flower bleeds beauty
a coyote cries

Shutters

"Weary, past midnight, who are you searching for?"
—Ho Xuan Huong

Shadows swim in the river of night.
Schools of light float around me.
This earth is small.
Is this my mother's womb
where I grew into black skin?
Where I increased the population
of Dawson to seven-hundred eighty-nine?
Where English wrote itself on my tongue?

In this chamber where I am lost,
there is a pigtailed girl.
Poverty beats against her lungs.
An ashy-kneed child who runs
from old men's catcalls,
chases adolescent boys.
A long-legged twelve-year-old bed wetter
who knows the feel of stone in her throat.

The barefoot daughter who wears the sting
and comfort of her mother's hand.
The ragdoll who bites the sheets
when the wind whispers
"It's because I love you."
She loathes the wind—
loves clothesline poles, tree branches, tall places,
to hear her mama sing "Amazing Grace"
when she's hanging out clothes.

Who is this stalk of sadness standing in the mirror
picking at tiny pubescent spots of shame,
wishing she were a sparrow or the ballerina
in a snow globe?

I want the woman who will not wear
fear as an overcoat, a refugee
from a rough past.
Who can see on this darkened road
where the horizon is an illusionist.
Where are the barrels of stars?

The large drinking gourd?
Where is the lady raving against the wind?
The one with the moon beating in her chest.

II. Blaze of Day

Blaze of Day

There is goodness in this blaze of day.
The way a pigeon perches on a nest of stones.
The way light draws a silhouette of its eye.
The way a stray tom ignores instinct,

retreats to a hammock of shade
stretched across a wooden fence.
The way the wind walks quietly
through the fruitless mulberry's branches.

A Sudden Blaze

(After Tony Hoagland)

*"Love is not a victory march it's a cold and it's a broken
hallelujah...."*
                                   —*Leonard Cohen*

Meet me where the sun loiters on hinge of sky,
where light has licked away layers of bushy darkness.

Meet me between the cold-faced house
with broken hallelujahs spilling out the windows,
between the hungry boy's bony bare shoulders,
between the memories of my ancestors chained ankles.

Meet me between Kobani and Bodrum's beach,
between anonymous faces floating in a fruitless channel
where the wings of twelve wounded birds stop flapping
in a dark wet limb of space.

Meet me between the slashed syllables
of in/ex/plic/a/ble

where shirts have no bones or flesh
to lift them from muddied water,
where refugees are treated like bombs.

Meet me under the fruitless mulberry
where the neon 7-11 sign sings its electronic song,
where the blue-eyed lady with the torn velvet coat
rants about kisses with violence, poverty, vigilance
between the flame and feather inked on her thigh.

Meet me where struggle is an evening meal,
and the condemned solicits cornflakes for breakfast.

Meet me between suddenly
and finally the filling of empty purses,
where humanity's compassion is in probate.

Between the air where some political pundits pimp
prejudice for profit.

Between the chamber and bullet of a black Kel-Tec PF-9
that snuffed out the life of a seventeen-year-old,

between the motives of a mother's $250,000
pay-out for "Murderabalia."

Meet me between the red-knuckled rage
of abused women and passing grief,
between their baptismal pool of tears.

Meet me where love is an emergency,
where peace wades through a warren of dreamlight,
where the prints of her bare feet are tattooed
on those souls who are willing to make a difference.

My Mother's Eyes

I fuss with supper
stuffed in white Styrofoam.
Mama parks her wheelchair
at the oak table.
Diabetes made her legs ghosts.
Both amputated below the knee.

She stares beyond the backyard,
cuddles inside her sweater,
hugs heat and layers of years
against the cliff of her breasts.
The distant gaze in her glaucoma eyes is her Oz.
This kitchen, my Kansas.

I feel myself whirling in a wind of desire.
I want to crawl inside her mind,
view her unwrinkled memories, see what reels
are spinning in the theater of her thoughts.

Is she a child running in a long field of wildflowers?
Bony body draped in a humble dress.
Hair styled in cornrows.
Face bumping against the sun's chest of heat.

Has she returned to the powdery-colored cotton
fields of east Texas where she moves
with a sack strapped around her shoulder?
Walking, bent, picking from open bolls,
singing in her soft soprano voice?
Singing until a crew of stars tunnels
through debris of darkness,
ignites small torches of light in a summer sky.

I feel her spirit sprinting, Going Up Yonder
with gates constructed of pearls,
walls crafted with jasper, sapphire,
streets paved with gold.

I want to write on the wide window,
Here is your Emerald City.

Come back. Sit with me in this moment.

I bump her chair with my knee.
"Do you want all shrimp?"

Summer

the smell of summer
sits on the kitchen table
beside the pepper

At the 4:00 Dance Recital

Dancing is laughter in her feet.
Delight a strong pulse.
With a hand to tummy
and a hand to air,
she puffs her cheeks, looks backstage,
attempts to mimic her teacher's movements.

When she crosses the length of the stage,
six bouncy-haired angels draggle behind,
then flap their winged-arms past her.
She is left alone, the spotlight her red god.
Light swims around her four-year old face.
She waves at the uncounted eyes adoring her,
drops her hands to waist, wiggle-dances toward the exit,
the taps on her shoes clicking loud kisses
against the smooth mouth of a hardwood floor.

Different

Max opens the book he calls memory,
peels tattered covers back.
His mind is a finger flipping
through the pages of time.
He flips over to age twelve
where he is swaddled
in a worn green comforter
stripping paint from the ceiling with his eyes.
Outside, other boys play football.

Curious how this day is book-marked
in his mind: the fever, the way he falls
asleep with a river in his hand.
Dry waves cover the streams of his lifelines.
Somewhere across the clouds
an arthritic musician licks the reed
of his honeyed clarinet.

Jesus in Cowboy Boots

For Colton Bilyeu

I don't know if it was a Tuesday or Wednesday
when dawn cracked the darkness
and fell into the wide open road of morning

a perfect offering,
like my friend's freckles son.

Veined with shadows of telephone wires
he slanted his face upwards,
shut his eyes, unsealed the smile on his lips.

Look, Mama. I'm Jesus!
With arms extended, his babyish body
was an imperfect crucifix.

Sun-spikes nailed his hands to air.
Cowboy boots anchored him
to the top of a slide.

Robed in his daddy's T-shirt,
his dispensation was tasting
the warmth of a blue west Texas day.

A skinny wind rose like an omen,
blew gently across his open hands
as light hung on him beneath an ebullient sky.

What Does a City Girl Know About Cowboys?

This morning I watch Sterling
in his spurless dust-colored boots,
sweat-stained felt hat, blue plaid shirt
aged rough hands
feed a fawn from a milk bottle.

His swollen knuckles scarred
from the heft of hard work.
Fifty years he's been waking long before light
fully stampedes across the day, to fix fences,
wean calves, harvest crops, haul manure.

I'm a city girl who ropes broken branches,
rides evening shadows, herds dead leaves.
What I know about cowboys
I learned from reading storybooks
and watching Saturday morning westerns.

I watch him stuff a red bandana in the back pocket
of well-worn jeans, walk past a weather-beaten barn,
climb into the cab of a pale-bodied pickup.
He drives down the graveled path with his wheels
tossing stones at the myths of my childhood.

A Dear John Letter On Behalf of My Dignity

In 1881, while serving at Fort Davis, Lt. Henry O. Flipper was dismissed from the Army. He wrote a letter to Representative John A. T. Hull, October 23,1898, in an attempt to clear his name. The letter asks Congress for "that justice which every American citizen has the right to ask. "In 1976, the Army granted him an honorable discharge, and in 1999, President Bill Clinton issued him a full pardon.

—Center for Legislative Archives

How does slavery smell?
Like everything
you do not want your children to hold.

I left the circumstances of my birth in Atlanta
to live with practitioners of prejudice at West Point.
Their moon-colored, ghost-colored, cotton-colored faces
were cities, cold citadels I avoided.
My skin was a wall they could not scale.

In the south, heat burned a black man's pride.
At the Point, ostracism was a weapon aimed at my ego.
Officers were not gentle men;
again and again they promoted
me to the rank of exclusion.
In class, I was crowded by inches of isolation.

At the Fort, my court martial was a plot
by brother officers to castrate my character.
Their words reeked with insults.
Even the blue mouth of sky gaped at their accusations.
My skin was a wall they kicked with hard heels of hate.

I'm not soliciting sympathy because of my color.
Because of my color, Lady Justice took off her blindfold,
unchained her scales, broke the blade of her sword across my back.
For years I have bled with dishonor.

How does a man bandage humiliation?
This letter is a plea to reinstate my pride with a pardon.
My name is a wall you can wash clean with the cloth of your pen,
John.

Stranded

"Give yourselves to the air, to what you cannot hold."
—Rainer Maria Rilke

On this hot spring afternoon, she stares out the window;
your name is quiet on her tongue.
Rain was loose with her favors this season.
A riot of bluebonnets and Indian Paint Brush stagger
across the Texas hillside; their petal-heads scream beauty.

She is stranded on an island of memory.
Marooned with thoughts of your head
thrusting through her thighs,
hands reaching for the lamp of morning,
and the earth swallowing your small coffin.
She watches others escape into the mocking horizon.
For three months the air was your playmate.
When she held you, you kicked-boxed
with its nitrogen filled stomach.

Your tiny fists curl into eternity.
She longs to feel your tears on her shoulders,
hungry cries echoing in the yawning loneliness of her ears.
She wants to walk the floors with you in her arms.
She will accept fatigue as companion if...
If only...

Little One, do me a favor.
Lose your forgiveness in the mouth of your playmate;
your mother needs to feel it.
She lives her life ashamed of happiness.
She lives her life clutching a memory she cannot hold.

The Colors of Want

I wish autumn was sleeping on my chest.
I wish I could go to Stowe, smell the fire-colored horizon.
Taste the air beneath a blood-struck sky.

I'm stuck in this green March day,
shamrock less, no hint of Irish in my blood.
A pot of words the gold at the end of my rain-softened hill.
Still might buy a lotto ticket after I leave this white,
white room of stirrups, plastic gloves, probing nurse.
I won't complain about waiting for the doctor.
Kat's daughter was air-lifted to Lubbock two days ago.
Her brain dammed with blood.

I know the luck of surviving pricks
of needles, prodding of hands, the pestering.
I know a telescope makes distant objects appear nearer,
the iris adjusts the amount of light reaching the retina.
I know the science of wanting
those things beyond the reach of painted nails.
To make bright the scumbled shade of longing.

Gratitude's a leprechaun. My eyes, brown telescopes, focus
on a Vermont brochure. Peacock trees feather hues
of ginger, harvest, crimson leaves across a slick page.

I fan the brochure. Gentle winds of colors blow.

Bantam City

Para-Para synchronized line dancing

Miss Spring skipped through my flowers, shaking her head
like a wet shaggy dog and raking her fingers
across my small share of the earth.
She scratched until flakes of green dandruff
flecked the sandy bed
and spilled onto its stone headboard.

Summer! There's a bantam city outside my patio door—
six foot blonde sunflower skyscrapers
with rough hairy legs and bushy coarse mops.
No intimidation in their buttery seedy eyes
as they stare into the sun weaving baskets of heat.
They do not blink at bees, squirrels, wrens
or ants tramping across dirty streets.

Conceited zinnia floozies hot and sassy
in their short crimson skirts. No shame
in the way they attract butterflies and allow hummingbirds
to serenade them. Oh, if they would learn modesty from the plump
marigold missionaries in a neighboring block, who offer up
hundreds of yellowing soft teeth in perpetual smiles of praise!

They do not bow their hardy heads while worshiping the sun.
How patient they must be to cohabitate with those
pink petticoated begonias—such drama queens, so demanding,
such whiners. "We want the canopied corner."
"More food. More water. We'll wither if we don't have these things."

See those neurotic morning glories creeping about?
They scale fences, walls, and the thick legs of moonflowers,
Para-Para showing off their agile long arms and pastel tattooed bodies.

Gangs of lilac, white and blue crowd against the city's stone gate
to cheer them on. Or maybe they are decoys sent to distract me
from opening this new package of gardening shears.

Snapshot

Sun's wide angle lens
captured Plaza Pond's
dehydrated face.
White rocks along its parched mouth
dried like decayed old teeth.
Its dusty cheeks desperate
for a long tongue of water.
Drought posed, pouted all summer
as the sun took selfies
on a wild imperfect field of yucca.

Motherhood

"A dark forest at the end of the world."
                                                    —Terry Ehret

To the lady who asked me in her broken English,
"Why you no have children?"
Fleshy acorns covered the ground of my womb,
became large trees.
Roots grew beyond their boundaries, fused together.
There was no room in the small dark forest of my body
for birth's mighty branches.
One day I slept the sleep of Snow White;
a doctor cut all the roots of my ancestral tree.
When the light kissed me awake,
the forest inside was dead, the blood river dried,
and my womb was a sky.
I adopted the stars.
Now, each night they crowd around my window
like eager children craving to return home,
waiting for me to bless each one with a name.

The Dry Side of Texas

For Larry D. Thomas

The rain clouds had a run-in with the wind.
The desert's dry tongue
wags for forty-four square miles.

At the edge of a wire fence,
an orange beetle slinks
across a rusty green beans can.

I watch an island of prairie dogs
burrow through the conclusion of day.
Jump at the sight of a bereaved rattler's skin

buried in a tomb of straw,
the spidery limbs of cracked sand
mulling on an empty lot,

and the red ant crawling in its tiny beauty
across a white picket of light
and through a temple of overgrown weeds.

Those who depend on the sun
do not see the dry full air as deficit:
the prickly pear in its sharp pink pride,

the yucca with its exotic pointed palms,
the purple sage with its flavorful long leaves
lifted like a poem offering to the sky.

Of Death and Water

Odessa yawns
three hundred days of sunshine
spilling from its dusty mouth.

This November morning is plucked
from the sunless sky's sixty-five count Crayola box.
I open my back door to find a leaking faucet
and the wind, with its coarse hands,
resurrecting dead leaves.

They ascend, reach for the balcony.
Too heavy for air to hold, they fall
into the burial ground of my backyard.

Startled by my breath's protest
against the cold,
my neighbor's gray cat rushes

across the open sepulcher.
How gentle the sound of death
against paws and fur.

How curious the way darkness pines for light.
How it wants to step out of its atomless body,
live in clouds of electrons.

How this dripping faucet wants
to be the Rio Grande with its voice
of stone and water singing across borders.

Before We Looked Up

For Janette Sloper

When the rain receded there was nothing left
except your ruffled voice.
"Look! Right through there. At the edge of that cloud,
you can see color; I think a rainbow is forming."

We'd seen rainbows even before we looked up.
A dingy orange and white donkey-shaped piñata
with severely pointed pale blue ears
strung on the ceiling of Lowe's Grocery Store
on South Clements Street,
green tree-brooches pinned on hills
between Sterling City and San Angelo, Texas,
a vase of yellow tissue flowers
at the Chinese Garden restaurant,
a smiling Buddha's red sash swayed
in the direction of a sign that read *pay here*.

We did— then walked into a humid Monday,
ignored its sundry hues,
their presence like nagging pigeons.

Listen to the Rain

Each drop sings
in its own language.
A million melodies
plummet to earth.

Beautiful
the way this liquid music
falls into a wet chorus of joy.

While Waiting at the Light

A godless wind leans against my Altima,
steel and flesh shake.

Lightning licks its snake-like tongue,
fear knots my throat.

Thunder scolds like a playground bully,
bladder tears wet my jeans.

After silence ripples across the sky,
I motor towards home.

In my rearview mirror—two rainbows;
my relief collides with their soft beauty.

Possession

Nine straight days of rain
have kept me from my evening walk.
I cannot collect the birds' conversations,
put them in my music
or count the paw prints from a cocky
gray tom who uses my car as a cot.

He lifts his back, makes an arch
of fur and bone,
restrains me with a stare
while he takes possession
of the horses sleeping beneath the hood.

Maxine Storm Watching

Her aged fists furl
into a fetal position
when lightning's long-limbed fingers
constantly scratch a contrary sky.

The wind, clumsy like beginnings,
stumbles over backyard furniture,
potted plants, a white plastic trash can.
Tree limbs shake like tambourines.

In the ruff music of the storm,
rain, like boots, stomps against windows—
a heavy rhythm in Maxine's fearful chest.
Curious, what she fears is what she saves.

Thunder ends its repine;
she swims in a deep channel of sleep.
How tender when silence swaddles
a fading gray sky.

How beautiful the patina of day
when morning's big hands cup leftover drops.
How wonderful the way last night's storm hides
in a withered leaf floating in the gully of a large bucket.

The Distraction at Target Shopping Center

is a replica of Venus. The curve of body, length of hair,
flawless skin, symmetry of face—perfect.
A bull's-eye in Target's Shopping Center.

She is the reason jealousy stitches tight seams
on the corners of women's mouths,
the reason worry grows in their stomachs.

I watch men watch her, their women watching them
watching her. All heads are pendulums
moving to the rhythm of her stride.

Relief, disappointment drop down from a ceiling
crowded with light when she throws her hair,
opens her arms, smiles, then scoops up the face of her face
from the young man charging forward, squealing "Mom---my!"

Maybe this Time Next Year

The July air lectures the sun on its modesty,
reprimands it for keeping temps below one hundred degrees.
What pressure to have your compassion questioned,
shamed for tucking the heat of your head
in the dark clouds.
It's been a long time since this West Texas sky
has worn such a gray top hat.
Maybe at this time next year it will wear a blue fedora.

I flush the generic aroma of antibacterial soap
from beneath my fingernails
like the sudden rain rinsing Odessa's dusty throat.
Maybe this time next year I will be a water lily
with light floating in my stomach.

I Am Rose

For David Meischen and Scott Wiggerman

"The plaintive courtship-themed 1853 lyrics of "The Yellow Rose of Texas" fit the minstrel genre by depicting an African-American singer, who is longing to return to "a yellow girl," a term used to describe a mulatto, or mixed-race female born of African-American and white progenitors. This iconic song of modern Texas and a popular traditional American tune, has experienced several transformations of its lyrics and periodic revivals in popularity since its appearance in the 1850s."
—The Handbook of the Texas Historical Association

This is what you'll find if you unzip history,
music pulsing in the cage of my ribs.
In the dark pipe of his longing,
my man makes a song for me.
White notes burst in his belly
when he thinks about the full nectar of my lips.

He keeps my name in the pocket of his tongue,
calls me his "yellow girl."
Anonymity doesn't keep me safe
from the long arms of lust.
My beauty is a magnet.

He sings of diamonds and dew;
the hard light of my eyes is a hammer
drumming against hungry hands
reaching to lift the skirt of my womanhood.

Heat climbs down the ladder of morning
three rungs at a time, descends on the day
with a heavy foot; he tells me he's leaving.
I listen to his reasons, promises of return.
My face waters with sweat, tears, knowing
I will not take him back into the folds of my love.

This quiet dusk I watch the sky float in the Rio Grande,
dream of the waves of muscles swelling
across his broad back, the camber of his mouth,
hard handsome face softening when he backs

away from me. I remember our fingers sliding
off the cliff of our grasp, the cavern of emptiness.

I shudder; the next touch will not be his.
I feel the petals of my want withering
along the pebbled-stone of distance.

Silk Flowers

Dawn's thin light sits
on summer's
green back.

She pulls
weeds, waters
geraniums.

I say *put
silk flowers
in the window.*
They are
manufactured
with life.

Their leaves
will not brown,
wither, fall—

unlike the ivy
sitting on
my kitchen table
dying from
silence.

The Eucalyptuses Stay

After the eucalyptuses
faded withered arms hang limp,
After they collect dust
in the centerpiece of magnolias,
After you criticize
the way I arrange my life,
After night ages into an albino sky,
and the geraniums smile red
in an infant morning,
After your desire for something
new replaces me as your fulcrum,
I will move on with the wind
and rake dead leaves from *our* garden.

In Defense of Harlots

"As an early frontier town, San Angelo was characterizedby
saloons, prostitution, and gambling."
—Texas State Historical Society

To fill their mouths
with the booze of derelict dreams
and smoky disappointments
is not their desire.

In their dim kitchens where purity is a dustless ledge,
dignity is timid candles.
They eat their tears,
listen to night's vanity.

They come with all they are in burlap sacks.
Find a land tented with fat weeds and skinny trees.
Hope as dwindling piles of poker chips.
Fate as a pair of loaded dice.

A swift roll— snake eyes.
They stare at the sky
watch life from their backs.
The vig of difficult beginnings—
the breaking and changing of lives.

I drink their sadness,
conceal their faces in an eddy of years.
The strong moon is my promise;
you will not remember them this way.

My throat is a memoir.
The tiniest secrets curl in me.
Decades are long rivers;
fourteen of them flow in the channel of my cheeks.

Their names are sealed in the smooth bellies
of river stones collected at the edge of your gardens.
The soft scent of lilacs is the memory
I leave drifting on the trail of their hard distant past.

River Stones

clustered like grapes,
a chorus singing
a wet requiem for summer.

For my thirtieth birthday
I received thirty
of their hard crooning cousins

huddled together
in a dusty vanilla ice-cream box,
each one bears a blessing in black ink.

I heft one of the singers,
press its rough jagged lifelines
against my smooth ones,

listen for the stone's melody.
It sits in my palm
immersed in silence,

its voice drowning
in the soft dry
folds of my flesh.

On The Way to the City of St. Francis

I move through the city of sky in rented steel wings,
touch fingers to glass, press towards a blue canopy
and avenues of rambling ashen clouds.

Embarrassed when a tide of heat
washes over me, wets my forehead.
I turn on a miniature box fan.

Curious how a chill can comfort.
Curious how chilled eyes can wound.
Curious how I apologize for who I am,

explain my suffering to relieve others
from the discomfort of my misery.

Recitation on Moving

Moving is a pair of sturdy hands with bruised fingers
kneading sunlight, washing windows with such joy
sweat rolls like wheels, like water
across the full warm body of day.

Day stepping out of its long steam bath
filling the horizon with smoky images
of my hands hauling away the last boxes.

My hands turn two keys.
One locking memories in the seams
of stained and cracked walls.
The other opening into a white canvas,
waiting for me to live what I can't imagine.

Speed Dating at the Desert Inn Poetry Café

This is a dream I can taste.
The sweat of beer bottles settles
at the bottom of orange plastic seats.
Velvety tongues of fire flap
from violet votive candles.
Air smells of the past's recycled smoke.

Pens poised,
we sit in the poetry café
clustered at round tables.
The almond-eyed, curly-haired,
bearded matchmaker balloons his arms,
parts them; pages of verse rain like confetti
into many reaching hands
and my lifeline buzzes
with apprehension.

Holding my breath,
I watch my poem flatten herself against the page
when a burly-chested sentence
from another poem leans too close.
She glimpses a G-string
limping up the small of his back—
glint, glimmer, glisten, gleam
on the band like four worn shoes.

Calm drifts over me when I see her
in the crib of soft fingers.
She smiles at a cowboy poet
with pale eyes and skin.
A big ADVERB medallion hangs
from his long neck; he playfully chants
"every tomorrow, seldom soon,
finally, my darling girl."

The night stretches like a long highway
before she returns to me, lumbering rhythms
balanced, awkward sentences fluid,
letters properly ordered in each word.
Sitting at an orange booth with the soft blade of my pen,
I delicately slice away the last bit of noise
so I can hear my poem singing.

Tumbleweed Two-step

Fingers of green split dirt
in my barren January garden.
Yesterday it was eighty.
Today the temp crashed to thirty-five.
How can a body not succumb to fever and flu?
How can a country not be sick with fear?

The wind choreographs cold rain.
Tires splash *chh, chh, chh* through puddles
and tumbleweeds two-step along a wire fence.
They rock side-to-side, roll, unsure
which one of them should lead.

Again we face the same mystery.
Hearts split into donkeys and elephants,
create a crater large enough to swallow friendships.

Coughing, I use a broken limb
to settle the present debate—
force those tumbleweeds forward,
make them move beyond complacency.

What Shall I Call This?

For my friend, Jax

A bird flapping
its wings in my throat,
beating its song into my voice
so I can sing its vision:

a naked summer sky,
mulberry leaves shaking
away the last dust of night—
you, walking towards me
in morning's long aisles.

Mischief loiters at your smile's edges.
A blood-colored chrysanthemum peeps at me
from the blinds of your fingers.
When I drape my hand over yours, I feel all the years
I've loved you rush into its soft, stout head.

III. Storms and Starlight

Storms and Starlight

The wind walks quietly
through the fruitless mulberry branches.
Orange-fingered flames press against windows.
Black petals of smoke drift towards the sky.

A dog barks; his throat clots with sorrow.
A parade of ashes march across the parking lot.
Who can hear the cadences of their apologies?
Overhead, tears of light fill a long corridor of stars.

Testimony of My Right Breast

This day knows it's a has-been,
dusky hands cling to the last ropes of light.

A large arm of orange grows across the sky,
stains the wide roof of Odessa.

Summer, this city is a chimney; heat burns
through the open flue of night.

A cocktail of Juniper Breeze and sweat
rolls across a budding tumor.

Wet beads trickle where the surgeon's scalpel,
chemo and rays of radiation will scar, scorch me.

This is my confession of hope,
not Emily Dickinson's feathered hope,

a muscled feral hope with powerful teeth to seize
and slice the flesh of this fierce fear roaming inside me,

I (will) live after the blade, drip of chemo, laser heat
singe, lump my skin. How does the left breast see me now?

My host sees a deformity; I am a redbird fluttering
in the rough hands of healing.

Descent

"Are you in love with these rivers and hills?"—
—Ho Xuan Huong

Moon, who knows the weight of time,
how day falls into night?
How long the epic of lack?

Yesterday evening was a half-crazed,
fully-famished coyote.
Its dried dusty tongue stabbed,
striking stone and bramble,
 at remnants of moisture.

Gray anorexic clouds spat
on the city with scattered showers.
Overnight, they grew fat
with extra water weight.

Then millions of wet crumbs descended
from the overstrained sky.
Like coyote, I howled with happiness,
while lack and moon vanished
behind the small hissing of time.

Homeless Man as Poet

October unbuttons his rumpled coat.
Leaves fall from high limbs
onto a cracked sidewalk.
A vortex of orange, pink and amber
whirls into the opening gate of night.

He stretches his mouth
with his forefinger and thumb.
He tells me, "This is an ocean.
My tongue swims in here.
Do you like it?"
An answer floats in my mind
before he interrupts my thoughts.

He points to a colony of stars.
"The sky loves the ocean.
You think the breeze of wind is an accident?
He seals a message in its breath.
He wants to give her violets.
Can you open the vault between them?"

"Hey! They won't let me in there."
He nods at the coffee shop.
I blink; a cup of hot Chai in hand
is evidence I am accepted.
He tells me *buildings are gods with windows for eyes.*
Sometimes they rupture the darkness
with a lamp silhouetted against the pane.

Small money and an illegible expression
is what I give him for his poem.
I watch him hobble
into a nebulous ocean of darkness,
a shadow cast between buildings that reject him.
Wind and night are the footprints he leaves behind.

I wish I had told him my body is an ocean
and loneliness swims inside.
I wish I had told him we are both leaves
fallen from the wide open mouth of a violet sky.

Offspring of Extremes

321 miles west of Fort Worth
and 280 miles east of El Paso, rests Odessa.
How many years have you been here?
Before steel horses dipped their noses
in your trough of sand and oil?
Before obese heat sat on your days,
corpulent chills covered your nights?
Before a desiccate sky left rivers of cracks
in the belly of your red earth?

How many years have you known
the stab of cacti, brutality of wind,
conversations of coyotes,
taste of the sagebrush's bitter juice?
My body is a desert, too.
It knows the oppressive burn of want,
the cold breath that swallows bloodlines,
the cracked earth of womanhood,
the brutality of...

In the cathedral of sky,
Night, with his broad-shouldered darkness,
takes Moon as wife.
This is love we both understand.
Stars, like leaves, feather her full white belly
and we, orphans of day, clutch
the clipped umbilical cord hanging
in the soft birthing room of her light.

The Close of Day

When the last patches of blue disappear
in the supple palm of night's charcoal hand,
bodies of celestial light become clear,
travelers in a heavenly caravan.

In the supple palm of night's charcoal hand,
a shawl of clouds brushes the moon's pale face.
Travelers in a heavenly caravan
unveil themselves with elegance and grace.

A shawl of clouds brushes the moon's pale face.
Cassiopeia and Orion
unveil themselves with elegance and grace.
Day ends with a gracious benediction.

Cassiopeia and Orion
bodies of celestial light become clear.
Day ends with a gracious benediction
when the last patches of blue disappear.

Distractions

"When someone dies, the clothes are so sad."
—Emily Fragos

Her closet is a distraction;
organization a soldier of her obsession.

The entire afternoon her hands take orders
and obey the combatant's stern commands.

When darkness marches across the sky,
garments hang on racks in platoons:

long, short, sleeveless
reds, whites, blues, blacks,

stripes, prints, dress, casual
her mood is not; she makes her tears roll upwards,

keep them behind the walls of her eyes,
continues sorting:

linen, denim, wool, twill,
cord, cotton, cropped, slacks

off she does not. She makes a nest of sweaters,
places coats in their plastic cocoons,

hangs belts from pegs like leather streamers.
Right below the hem of her dresses

a box crammed with every poem
her son penned since he was old enough

to hold a pencil, before he put on a uniform,
before he was deployed, before his casket

was clothed in the American flag.
She shoves the box into a corner,

leaves it in the dark hole of neatness.
Behind the closed door, a clutter of blocky letters

cram joyful verses
in the seams of her somber clothes.

Destiny

Stretches her body
in the long black leotard of night,
untangles her ancient braids.
An insomniac for ages,
she thinks of that astute animal—
the unknown.
She knows in the woods of mystery
the darkest of hidden things keep moving
toward long leaves of light.

Last Thursday

The sky is a woman.
Silent now.
Her old stories are written in the constellations.
She stares in the white pond of moon,
a dark turban of night on her head.
Complexity is her mirror.
Of all the wonders of this world,
she is the most ancient of mysteries.

She can cleanse the earth
with a lift of her skirt,
split calm open with chaos.
Her life is as long as the beginning;
she floats beyond the wicket of time.

Her morning eye, bright with the known
and unknown, stares down at waves
of colorful faces rowing beneath her.
The boats of their bodies are burdened
with dark and beautiful cargo.

This Thursday afternoon,
Ambreen's sixteen-year-old body,
is bound and set ablaze for love.

Her mother and brother give their blessings
as fire leap-frogs through pools of petrol.
A van, her tomb, burns with tradition
as tongues of fire lick her bones,
anda full mouth of smoke sucks her breath.

Could they hear the flesh of their flesh
crying, begging escape from the flames?
Were their ears plugged with customs?

Are their hands made of stones?

When the ground is a cold pillar of her memory,
she is a lone white dove
flying into the ancient arms
                    of mother sky.

Driving

The road is a house.
A wall of eighteen wheelers
scuds along West Interstate 20,
barricades two lanes.
Big black tires peel loose pebbles
like old paint.

The road is a boomerang.
Small stones ricochet
off my car's windshield,
miniature mallets tapping
a warning melody on glass.

The road is a U-Haul trailer
dragging furniture, totems, lives
from one end of existence to the next.
Wheels wobble, burdened with obsessions.

Sleep is a road my body wants to travel.
Weariness lifts its heavy thumb,
hitchhikes on my neck.
I blink my eyes like slow wipers.
Night is a crow. Its dark wings swoop
over my Altima's red hood.
My lights slash through its soft feathers.

Fear is a seatbelt,
keeps me fastened inside the car
when I pass a rest stop.
What's there or what's to come
scarier than my head bobbing beneath
a sky seeded with stars.

Ode to Buzzards

> "We just wanted to be alone in that great shining emptiness."
> —Arthur C. Clark

Buzzards circle on Highway 158
outside of Garden City, Texas
where emptiness' face is miles of scruffy fields.

Beyond a bouquet of mesquite bushes,
an animal's torn flesh and bones
are offerings on death's altar.

I dare not slow my car
for the sake of identity or call death
my lover.

It hangs around like a devoted dog.
Hangs onto careless proclamations.
"This, whatever this is, will be the death of me," I say.

Death rips the words from my tongue,
hangs them on chance's door hinges
mulls them over in its dark cape.

I track its movements
from the dust-ridden desert floors of West Texas
to the turtle pace of Clear Creek's
green waters where streaks of sun curl
around the large blond beak of a Great Blue Heron.

Great Blue hammers the waters,
nails death in the sharp bones of a perch.
At the edge of the creek, light is a wide hat.
Its brim covering a tiny island of small white rocks
shining like a set of freshly bleached teeth.

Tuesday's Sky

Sunday was drowning in sunshine. Monday morning the glass patio
    doors
were museum walls with the sun hanging like a van Gogh.
Tuesday's sky hoarded dark clouds, trashed both the morning and
    afternoon
with heavy sheets of rain. I watched it across three hundred sixty-six
    miles.
The car's thin-armed-wipers worked overtime sweeping my windshield.
I stopped at a *Town and Country*, bought a burrito, stared into the
    drizzle
as I refueled my car. Not wanting to think about what was ahead,
I steered my thoughts through the vista of memory,
back to a day when rain held us hostage to the indoors.

It was summer. My brothers, the superheroes, and I, the brooding
    preadolescent,
watched Mom stretch pink strips of bacon into an old black cast iron
    skillet.
Grease sputtered and hissed incantations until the bacon was crisp and
    brown.
With hurried hands and little boy accuracy, my younger brothers dipped
a butter knife into the mayo jar. Side-to-side the dull blade danced
over two slices of bread. They built their BLT's with tomato
and wet limp lettuce. At the table, they sat with bath towels draped
    down
their backs—their rendition of Superman's cape. Full, they flew
to the living-room to watch their favorite superhero; they did not
    witness him
save Metropolis. Rain, that liquid Kryptonite, weakened them,
made them powerless in the villainess hands of sleep.

Looking Up Through the Fruitless Mulberry

"When darkness makes a place at the table,
I feed him and teach him what hospitality feels like."
                                    —Adriene Crimson Coen

Darkness is a bully by birth.
No one taught him tenderness.
When he broke the wings of your longings,
he taunted you with dreams.

Sometimes you have to let desires sleep.
Sometimes you have to treat emptiness like a friend.
Sometimes you have to gather light from the hem
of a closed door.

Out of kindness, the universe hangs lanterns
on the darkened street of your heart
but will not always give you what you demand.

I feel you fumbling through the house,
your yearnings strong enough to break windows.
Wishes are fragile glass.

I watch you walk across the yard,
look up through the dense roof
of the fruitless mulberry.
The leaves are ventriloquists.
Their voices tremble
with your melancholy in the long evening.

Tears are words, too.
Your eyes write on the slate of slanted sky
everything you are not saying.

Winter's Princess

"Neither be cynical about love – for in the face of all aridity
and disenchantment it is perennial as the grass."
—Max Ehrmann

When I said, *you will be back*
you laughed at me like my sister—
that pesky harlot wind lifting her skirt
before summer's generous eyes.
She makes this day dizzy with her flirting;
it spins heat like a whirlpool.

Evening, I hear the pines outside my door rubbing
their branches together in victory after snagging her hem.

It's September. She bewitches fall—
whistling, dancing as it takes her in its chilly arms,
caresses her emptiness, chatters with her cruelty.
You say you love the wind; is it her guile?
You are the wind, think I'm a generous summer,
a dizzy blue day spinning in heat for your love.

But I am winter's princess—cold and hard.
I will not melt under the heat of your voice
when you call, crooning like the wind,
singing fall's first scarlet song.

A Postcard from My Mirror

"Maybe you are searching among the branches for what only
appears in the roots."
                            —Rumi

I was not there
when you were a pea of clay
in the earth of your mother's womb.

The sky is a sideshow.
Stars, those naked celestial officers,
ornament its deep channel of darkness.

You stare at them to avoid me.
I do not tell you what you want to see.
You are a freckle in sky's doorless house.

I, unlike a poem, am not the eye
that sees the foundation
beneath your house's skin.

Your trips to me are seldom.
I do not miss your visits.
I write to inform;

each time you give me your back,
I watch the dim room
mop up the lamp's static shadow.

Foreign Body

When I see my naked shadow on the wall,
I want time to redress itself.
This skin scares me.

I can carry a symphony in my belly.
It used to fit a combo; I want the jazz.
Let me squeeze inside the diminished chords.

I can't understand this new flesh.
Give me back the riffs in my legs,
the be-bop of my hands.

Dawn breathes hard when it wakes,
the breeze sounds like a barking dog.
I want to go back to sleep.

This body has too many secrets.
Too many scars
to eat these tender seeds of light.

Bring back the covers of darkness.
Let the stars hum across the sky.
Let me sing with my eyes.

Voyeur

Oh, this appetite for flesh and splendor!
Shirtless, he taps a pair of tongs against his thigh, licks the lip
of a salty-mouth glass, stares beyond me—my want.
Whiffs of charcoal and smoked beef blow
across ripples of hard muscles.

I watch, desire dancing in my stomach
red-flamed tongues bussing in his barbeque grill.
Next year at this time, I will have known many meals;
this heat, lust for my bronzed *David's*
steaks will be lean memories.

When night unfurls a chilly carpet of air,
I slink inside, close the blinds,
shut-out a blizzard of stars blowing
across the broad darkening desert sky.

When I Flipped the Switch

"I'm restless. Things are calling me away.
My hair is being pulled by the stars again."
—Anais Nin

to the ceiling fan, its domed machetes slashed
the jungle of darkness in my bedroom;
the windmill-blades spun a monotone melody
on the rim of my empty cup.

My eyes traversed to the clock on the nightstand.
12:01AM. No metamorphose!
Where was the magic of midnight?
Was it, too, a lost illusion?

I had not become Diana, goddess of the moon,
or one of the stars in her harem.
My body remained a long frame of flesh.
The stars made the darkness tremble
on the ink-black plate of sky,
but their throats were too small to swallow it.

The weight of the cup against my palm
reminded me of its emptiness.
I returned to the kitchen to fill it.
The hair on my arms and neck were like cold small feet.
I felt the chill of their steps when I flipped the switch.
When I glanced back, I saw light from outside the window
leak a small puddle on the edge of the yawning sink.

Transformation

Sun stretches
across redwoods
like a violin string.

Light plays a concerto.
Evening plods up day's long stairs,
draws the blinds.

A block of blackness
fills the spot where I stand.
Moon attempts to shine

her flimsy beam
around dark edges.
Destiny tells me who I was

was good enough for the time
I was *that* woman;
stop lamenting her.

I am a violin string, too.
The woman I am now
is not the woman

I will always be.
With each song of day,
I must be re-tuned.

Night Alley

Night is a wide dark fence
posted around the city.
I ride around its boundaries
with the car window cracked
listening to the radio harmonize
with the wind, dogs and my engine.

At the stop sign near home,
I decide against the shortcut
and stretch the drive a few more feet.
Though I am shielded by tons of steel,
fear is the rusty latch that locks
me out of a dirty alley.

When I get ready to turn,
a wiry silver-haired woman shepherding
a Target shopping cart
trundles into view.

Her metal buggy burdened
with bags of clothes,
dented cans and mystery items
only she and the stars know.

Raising the window and fencing out her courage,
I watch her from the review mirror unlock
the rusty latch and walk into that place I feared.
I drive on with her back whispering in the distance,
feel the blood rise in my face
as the sound of her cartwheels pulsate in my bones.

50 Boulevard Voltaire

"On the day after Armistice Day in 1918,
Monet promised his homeland a "monument to peace"
in the form of massive water lily paintings."
                         —Kristy Puchko

Red in its liquid sneakers runs over stones and flesh.
Security's ribs crack.
Music smells of blood and gunpowder,
tastes like fear's sweat.

Monet's Paris drowns in sorrow.
Each cuplike flower of the *Water Lilies*
overflows with brutalities humans heap
upon other humans.

What monument shall we offer
the afflicted, the fragmented, the exiled?
The white Frisbee moon suspended in a sad sky?
The trembling air's plethora of prayers?
A bouquet of compassionate hands?

Wind, do not walk gently on those crushed roads of humanity.

Yesterday When the Flag was Silhouetted Against the Moon, I Forgot a Young Soldier's Name, But I Remembered His Eyes

They were nets, snared me to my relic of a chair.
Last year he was at the prom with his high school sweetheart.
Last night *he* looked handsome in his military uniform.
Nineteen, on the evening news, an America hero.
In two years, had he lived, he could rent a car.
Private?
Couldn't remember his name; it scrolled beneath his picture.

Uniforms, names, young men faces,
flag silhouetted against the moon.
I scanned some of their obituaries in the local newspaper,
saw pictures posted on church bulletin-boards,
ate in restaurants where their smiles hung from walls.

On the front page, I read about a couple who lost two sons in Iraq.
saw their grief stricken faces.
They held framed photos of their two uniformed sons.
Who could console? No one could return them;
the moon could not mop up their blood.

I pleaded absolution with the stoic glass
that so quickly flashed pictures like yours:
young man, forgive me
for not remembering your name.
So quickly war pilfered your voices.
There were so many like you.

When Big Red Tastes Like the One You Can't Forget

Her anger lives in the taking:
death whirls him away before she can protest.
His razor stubble is ruff feathers against her ear
until morning drags sleep from her eyes.
Day washes away her dreams
like the last load of his clothes she laundered.
His overalls are scented with Tide. How she longs
to hold the smell of his musk and grass-stained cloth.
She would settle for her body against his shadow;
death took that, too.

Loneliness pushes her out of the sad house.
She drives to the Music City Mall,
perches on a bench near Burlington Coat Factory,
ignores the constant stream of people surging pass,
stares at dark-haired twins playing in a green water fountain.
They taunt a smiley blow-up replica of Shamu
the whale, and a blue polka-dot octopus—
run to their daddy's arms.
Their three-year old faces mirror joy.
He scoops them up; they are fins on either side of him.
Gleeful squeals bubble in their tiny throats.
The three of them drift away in their happiness.
She knew joy like this when her husband held her hand.

Denial is an ogre of yellow leaves piled in the backyard,
fear is a tiny bell trilling in the stomach,
and light cannot crawl its way out of darkness.
There was never a blueprint for a life without him.

After Pneumonia Seals Your Eyes

Outside, rain cries on the stained-glass windows.
I grip the side of your casket,
try to squeeze my life into you.

This November day is full of sad rhetoric.
Voices like metal pots clang in my ears,
Let go. We need to close the coffin.

I move my hands away from the box
that has no room for me.
Watch white-gloved hands lift you into a black hearse,

wheel your body away. I do not follow—
not ready for the earth to take you,
hold you against my will.

Today, I write a poem for you,
scribble your plot number at the bottom of the page—
a map to the place I have no plans to visit.

Thursday Night Poetry Reading

I am the lone ambassador of poetry
before a delegation
of the Thursday Night Writers Group.
They stare, pencils posed on the page.

The president admonishes although I am a poet
they can still learn from me.
How genuine her belief, beautiful her cause,
sad her explanation.

Before sharing *Why Write Poetry,*
I read my first poem.
It's an anthem of protest for the man
sitting on the second row.

There's no gage to measure
the swell of hostility in his voice,
That's not a poem. It doesn't rhyme.
I do not tell him there's no rhyme

for an orange soaked sky at the end of an idle day,
no end-stopped for a candle's hot tongue
burning scents of lavender into its smooth body.
The wind's not dactyl when it scraps wispy arms

on the aged bare branches of a chilly maple.
Maybe there is a spondee
in the smile-smothered face
of a cancer patient holding

her grandchild for the first time.
His face is a billboard of disapproval,
azure eyes commercials of complaint,
crossed arms empty pens.

The words pitching from my larynx
are more determined
than his
angry stone stare of disagreement.

In the Deep

"When a young, free-swimming male angler encounters a female,
 he latches onto her with his sharp teeth.... A female will carry six or
more males on her body."
                              —National Geographic

After the sun slouches below the bargeboards
of the sea's wide house,
After its huge bottom dips below the intricate blue
waves sprawling with mystery,
After it squeezes its generous body
through balusters of darkness,
After it sinks down into the deep treads of the deep
where light is a thin reed,
where love is a parasite with razor teeth,
with all things male clinging, fusing, dissolving
into the blood and skin of a harlot
pimped out by the brutality of the sea.

Under the Hood of Night

Drought is an unwelcomed camper
in this far away city.
It haphazardly empties its knapsack
filled with dry heat and weeds,
pitches a tent with new water restrictions
as its pegs.

A whip of sound, disturbing
as a sudden siren's wail,
shoves me into the shadows
of my dreams. My heart shudders
with fear. I take deep breaths,
try to rein calm into my body.

My window is a partition
between my cotton-throat silence
and the intruder of my sleep.
Bravery— a peek through slits
in the olive-colored curtains.

The church of sky is filled
with drifting planets, darkness
and pews of stars. My neighbor hides
his deeds under the hood of night.
His water sprinkler floods
his barely blond-tipped grass.
How ungodly, this hose-rain!

How can he rationalize his fat bushes,
the rabble of green? Explain the need
for his rock-tossing lawnmower
to neighbors whose lawns feast on a diet of dust?

I sit at the table in my rainbow-colored T-shirt,

cream-colored pajama pants, in search of a cheese
enchilada recipe and the ethics of this late night.
Do I report his rebellion or say prayers of thanks
for this unlawful patch of beauty
teasing through the brown world of our street?

Night Ritual

Each night the moon pole-vaults over the wall of the horizon.
Each night the stars tell it you can't.
The wind turns its head.
A mesquite opens its muted mouth
while darkness swabs its dry throat.

Strangers Anxiously Waiting for Me to Finish So They Can Fly into Their Dreams

For University of Texas of the Permian Basin Fall Class of 2016

I try to imagine you
in the soft fabric of this day.
Your black robes, temporary wings
trembling on the air of joy.
Your faces as changing as clouds
drifting across the sky of my imagination.

I must have a name for what I store
in the basket of my mind, name you Destiny.

Here you are waiting for your diploma,
the gold-sealed ticket
that will give flight to your dreams.
How will you fill the space
when they are fluttering in the gale
of your future?
Will you lecture morning
with its ragged silver light
about perpetual beginnings
and early starts?
Will you shave the dark edges of night
with the sharp wit of your plans?

What can I give you to hide
in the pocket of your memory?
Life's big sister, Wisdom?
It's strong nail, Truth?
Dreams are hard masters

with unrelenting demands.
If you bow beneath their heavy hands,
know there is beauty in humility.
Courage in letting your heart walk alone
in the wide unkempt field of the unknown.

Desert Light

> "... suddenly, there: a gate into such distances as perhaps only birds know..."
>
> —Rainer Maria Rilke

A wren chirps on a gate
stretched between night and dawn.
A small chorale of clouds sings
morning is here with her long burning candles.
How lovely the soft music of light
pulsing in the voice of this desert sky.

The last remnants of darkness disappear.
On my block, houses wake and brush
their windows in daylight.
The air tastes like new beginnings.
A fly, that symbol of unwanted things,
beats hard against the pane.

Is this not true of the desert sun
when it beats against the pane of our bodies?
Heat a pumice against the skin.
Flesh and glass both fragile.
Vulnerability is our light.

Curious how the harp of dusk strums
a pink cadenza just as we desire
shadows smaller than ourselves.

Night in its wisdom shuts its ears.
Stars, those tiny crumbs,
leave a trail of silence.

Three Sisters

I Dawn

An exiled windmill stares,
refuses to turn its head
as dawn, light's chaste sister,
streaks sky's soft upper lip with orange.

Dew falls on the red *Radio-Flyer*
that waits for children who will not return.
The air sweetens its breath with honeysuckle.
There is goodness in this break of day.

II Blaze of Day

There is goodness in this blaze of day.
The way a pigeon perches on a nest of stones.
The way light draws a silhouette of its eye.
The way a stray tom ignores instinct,

retreats to a hammock of shade
stretched across a wooden fence.
The way the wind walks quietly
through the fruitless mulberry's branches.

III Storms and Starlight

The wind walks quietly
through the fruitless mulberry's branches.
Orange-fingered flames press against windows.
Black petals of smoke drift towards the sky.

A dog barks; his throat clots with sorrow.

A parade of ashes march across the parking lot.
Who can hear the cadences of their apologies?
Overhead, tears of light fill a long corridor of stars.

CPSIA information can be obtained
at www.ICGtesting.com
Printed in the USA
FFOW03n1051160917
39899FF